OF BONE, OF ASH,
OF ORDINARY SAINTS

PRAISE FOR
OF BONE, OF ASH, OF ORDINARY SAINTS

Do yourself a favor: Open this book and read "The Infrequent, Yet Beautiful, Trumpeters." That's what you hold in your hands. That's what you're about to fall in love with. Gailmarie Pahmeier transports us to the state of Nevada with poems layered in historical context, while also serving as a witness to the extraordinary lives of those who rarely find themselves in verse. Pahmeier asks us to "consider all the ashes you are asked to carry" while reminding us that "the last voice / you'll hear is one singing, barely a whisper." What begins as an obvious love song to the state of Nevada ends as a love song to the strangers who pass through our lives, beautiful and hurt and tenacious in their quiet love for this world.

—**Brian Turner,** Director of Sierra Nevada University MFA Program, author of
Here, Bullet and *Phantom Noise*

Gailmarie Pahmeier's *Bone and Ash and Ordinary Saints: A Nevada Gospel* takes readers on a cinematic road trip through rural Nevada with a narrator who knows how to tell a good story, knows just the right thing to say, and when to say nothing and simply listen. Along with the coyote, deer, owl, and other wildlife, the book is populated with dogs—the dog with sunglasses and a top hat, a German shepherd who's a good kisser, hounds, chihuahuas, border collies—but encircling them all is the spirit of the "one great dog" who journeys through these poems, as the narrator scatters his ashes over various sites, recognizing what is holy in each, blessing them with a guardian. Gailmarie finds *the lovely* in *the lonely* old roads. She observes, "what we love most remains / communal, as common as a kiss." If the bittersweet humor of the parks and people featured in these poems doesn't break your heart into beautiful pieces, the empty paint can in the end surely will.

—**June Sylvester Saraceno,** author of *Feral, North Carolina, 1965* and
The Girl from Yesterday

With grace and intelligence and wit, these luminously detailed poems drive us across Nevada and into the ancestral soul of its landscape and its people. Earthy yet reverent, effortlessly lyrical, these are poems that understand the path to the universal is through the regional. Each poem seems a lesson in empathetic observation: Pahmeier allows the voices of her "ordinary saints"—park rangers and waitresses, retired linemen and bewildered fathers—to sound clearly through her poems without sentimentalizing or degrading. The result is a "pure covenant" between poet and subject, between inner feeling and external landscape. Simply put, these are poems that know what matters and—because of this—matter.

—**Steve Gehrke,** author of *Michelangelo's Seizure*, selected for the
National Poetry Series

This book should be mandatory reading for every visitor to and resident of Nevada. A brilliant celebration of Nevada's state park system, a travelogue of Nevada's beauty, the rangers keeping it so, and the travelers passing through. There's a reason Pahmeier was the first poet laureate of Reno, Nevada. My favorite poetry book of the year.

—**Willy Vlautin,** author of *Don't Skip Out on Me*, PEN/Faulkner finalist

For years—decades, actually—I have looked to Gailmarie Pahmeier's poetry to instantly wake me like a splash of high Sierra spring water. Reader: brace yourself. This delight-laden and unforgettable book is just going to reach out and grab you, and then never quite let you go. Yep. That good.

—**David Lee,** former Utah Poet Laureate, Pulitzer Prize nominee, author of *Mine Tailings*

OF BONE, OF ASH, OF ORDINARY SAINTS

A NEVADA GOSPEL

POEMS BY

GAILMARIE PAHMEIER

WSC PRESS - *Wayne, NE*

ISBN 978-1-7320275-6-5
Published by WSC Press

Edited by Stepha Vesper
Cover and layout design by Chad Christensen
Cover photographs by Don Berinati

WSC Press
1111 Main Street
Wayne, NE 68787

wscpress@wsc.edu
WSCPRESS.COM

Dedicated to the Memory of Two Extraordinary Nevadans:

Kirk Robertson (1946-2017)
&
Joe Crowley (1933-2017)

TABLE OF CONTENTS

OF BONE, OF ASH,
OF ORDINARY SAINTS

First Saint Sighting, Las Vegas, 1969

We'd saved for the promise of Disneyland,
first family trip outside of Missouri,
long days in the hot car, treats of gum
and grilled cheese at truck stops. So much
to look forward to, our new shoes, hair bows.

But California's covenant of ease,
of dappled dreamland, startled and unsettled,
the relentless madness of spinning
teacups, our scuffed patent leather shoes
blistering our feet, and the heat, the heat.

I took refuge in the Tiki Room,
then the auditorium with the Lincoln
robot, the quiet magic of the nearly
real man, spent most of my savings
in air-cooled shops. These graces were enough.

Homebound, Las Vegas, our father played poker,
his one indulgence a few hours
in a dark and temperate casino.
We girls walked Fremont Street with our mother,
gazed into windows. So much. Such shine.

And then I saw it, the slender black
cigarette holder, silver mouthpiece,
imagined the hands who'd hold this.
While my sisters twirled under the neon,
I slipped into the shop, asked how much.

Five dollars. I had closer to three.
When the clerk asked why I wanted this,

I pointed toward my mother, smoking
on the corner in her faded green capris,
tight turtleneck, her face tired and plain.

The clerk reached into the window, pulled
the holder from its dusty display stand.
Our hands touched. *Close enough*, she said.

PART ONE

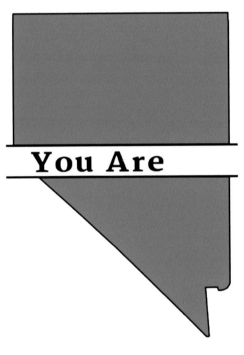

You Are

Guido: Have you ever been outside Reno, Ms. Taber?

Roslyn: Once I walked to the edge of town; doesn't look like there's much out there.

Gay: Everything's there!

Roslyn: Like what?

Gay: The country!

Roslyn: Well, what do you do with yourself?

Gay: Just live.

Roslyn: How does anyone "just live"?

from *The Misfits*, 1961

Naming Her

We knew the trailer was a woman,
the curvaceous frame, all thirteen feet
of white, of silver, of red the color
of his mother's lipstick, 1946.
Our girl was no vintage beauty,
but because her red reminded him
of the courage, tenderness, tenacity
of the single mother in the long gone
rural town, her shame palpable and hard,
we tried the old names first. Mabel, Ethel,
Edith and Myrtle. Harriet and Bess.
Constance and Florence. Charlene.

Nothing fit until we thought of Marilyn,
that Marilyn, her time here in Nevada,
her fraught performance in *The Misfits*,
that dress in the Dayton scenes, the ripe
red cherries patterned against the white,
the silvering of her hair in the stark sun
of this state. We named the trailer Roslyn.

Driving the Gone Dog Across Nevada

Everyone who's ever loved a dog knows
you get one great dog. The rest are good dogs.
We have good dogs now, a quick-witted pit
and a silly-sweet Jack and Labrador mix.
But the great dog is dead. For seven years
his bone bits and ash filled an old paint can
atop the washing machine. Where would he rest?

Our simple plan—the old truck and a secondhand
trailer, the dog in his can snug behind the seat.
We'd leave pinches of him at nearly every stop,
know where to find him if we needed to,
know that we'd left him to guard whatever
needed guarding—wild horses, turkeys,
owls, deer, the young woman alone,
the old man with the veteran's pass,
the family on the way to somewhere new,
somewhere better, somewhere with work.

I know what you're thinking, that everyone
who's ever loved a dog has a story,
a wholly sentimental one that may
likely include a road trip, grilled meats,
a car, a truck, a camper, some stars, a moon.
And you'd be right—what we love most remains
communal, as common as a kiss.

The West Side of Eastlake

Enter here. Fees are reasonable.
Toilets flush, shower stalls are tiled,
the hopeful neon of Reno near enough,
the purring rumble of highway traffic
assurance enough that others have somewhere
they might need to be. Few hours pass
without a plane above. You remember
all the times you've flown over this lake,
thought *I'm almost home*. There was always
someone waiting, someone who loved you,
someone who was uncertain you'd land safely.

Visitor's Guide: Washoe Lake State Park

The name comes from the tribe, families who spent winters in the lowlands of what is now Washoe Valley.

Oregon, Nevada, Illinois, Idaho... not a single vanity plate. Consider this.

When the mining boom was over, the towns around the Lake were abandoned. Most who remained turned to ranching, displacing the tribe from the Valley.

Consider.

In the wake of the rapid urbanization of nearby Carson and Reno, the park is a true treasure. Hunting with a shotgun is permitted in specified areas.

Where will we go? Where have you been?

This park promotes Leave No Trace Outdoor Ethics: Leave what you find. Dispose of waste properly. Respect wildlife. Be considerate of others.

Consider. Consider all the ashes you are asked to carry.

Walking the Loops at Washoe

Some have certainly settled in, hang clothes
newly washed at the pumps, string lines
from the trees—socks, shorts, a frilly blouse.
Others are more truly there for one night,
no tent, no camper, no noise other than
the sizzle of suppers, the long hiss
of wetted charcoal. It's the settlers
who surprise, their lawn chairs and little dogs,
their private need. You walk so you can know

the couple from Idaho who brews
their morning coffee in the public bath,
loves their fat chihuahua named Snickers
for his dark caramel coat and the way
he sneers a sort of smile. They arrive each
summer in their Crown Vic, set up their tent,
see the doctors at the VA. The man's older,
took up dying, cancer, three years ago.
Each year he requests an overstay, tells
the ranger he wants to die here holding
his wife and his round dog. Doctors, he says,
change opinions often, but he's not about
to take crap from anybody, if he can tell
it's crap in time not to take it. His wife
has smooth skin and the blackest hair
she brushes and brushes all day. Her smile,
like Snickers', curls, is quick. She never speaks.

You know the girl who comes in alone,
her small red car sparkling in the heat.
She unpacks her suitcase, cooks dinner,

is careful to kill the coals before she beds.
She's lovely, all angles. She makes calls
each evening, her voice no more than mere breath.
She's gone all day, returns at dusk, begins
again to call and call. Does she work
in Carson City? Is she waiting for
a place to truly park, to take her trunkful
of things, a place she can make her now home?
On the third night of calls, she suddenly stops
moving, quickly clears her camp, dumps
ice everywhere. She leaves. She doesn't return.

You know the middle-aged man in the vintage
teardrop trailer, Oregon plates. He's been
coming down to see his daughter every
summer at her community college
in Reno. He's missed her much, she's all
he's got besides his trailer and the work
he gets some seasons. Three years ago
he thought of moving here, of joining
her, of becoming Nevadan. But the rents
got high, higher, and he can't decide how
or where to live. The money's better here,
his daughter just graduated, got him on
with her at Chewy. They'll share this summer
together, then he's off to pick beets.
That's good pay, good work if you like it hard.

You walk to know these stories, to tell them.
At your own campsite, you'll cook chicken,
roast the requisite marshmallow, listen to

Johnny and June coming in from the Valley,
new neighbors setting up, the nostalgic scent
of their cigarettes, weighty as your own ash.
Man says *After this break, I'll put up the awning,
then after my next break, I'll set out the chairs.*
You'll sit out for hours in your own chair.
You know how quickly what passes goes past.

Visitor's Guide: Dayton State Park

Once a Paiute meeting place, base camp for fishing on the Carson River, and in winter, a shelter camp from the snows of nearby Sierra. The discovery of silver and gold changed that forever. (Plants, animals, artifacts, rocks and minerals are protected by state law. Please leave them where you find them.)

Please leave.

In the 1850s, camels were tested by the U.S Army for use in caravan operations. Experiment was unsuccessful. The camels were brought to Dayton to haul wood and salt to the mills and mines. These camels were later abandoned to fend for themselves. Few were seen after 1880. (Pets are welcome if on a leash in populated areas.)

Hold tight.

Dayton was the Lyon County seat until 1909 when one of the frequent—and often suspicious—fires burned the courthouse. Disastrous fires in 1866 and 1870 wiped out most of the town. The mill, too, was destroyed by fire in 1882 and again in 1909. Floods also took their toll. (Fires are allowed only in the provided fire rings and barbeque pits.)

Ashes, ashes…

Note to Willy from Dayton

Thanksgiving Eve and we are here, sipping
whiskey and thinking of you. Weather's mild
and tomorrow we'll host the holiday,
friends from Reno. I think you'd like it here.
This morning our campsite surrounded
by mustangs, hoot of an owl and howl
of coyote. We're reading your new novel,
love its pain and heart, how deftly you've
realized this state, our fragile wavering,
dread, delight, dread, delight. And dread again.
Good work, my friend. Tonight we'll watch the final
episodes of *Longmire*, indulgent pleasure
you, too, share. Your crush on Vic will remain
a secret, as long as you don't tell anyone
I'm in love with Longmire, his knuckle hair,
his lodge rug chest, his way of walking
that says, *I don't need to get there first,*
I just need to get there.

Roadrunner Café, Dayton, Nevada

Day after Thanksgiving, your friends gone home,
the leftovers left behind, pecan and sweet
potato pies given to the ranger.
He's grateful for these treats, his holiday
dinner eaten alone, your invitation declined.
He lives all year in the park, has a spot
under the oldest cottonwood. You ask
about breakfast, and he recommends
the Roadrunner. *Thick bacon, fresh eggs.*

The waitress has her arms full of platters,
eggs in all their many glories, bouquet
of sausage and the promised bacon, wedges
of orange, sprigs of parsley. More potatoes.
You will thank the ranger for this place,
for its dusty leatherette booths, its music.
When the waitress brings your order, she's swaying
along to Steve Miller—*really love your peaches,
wanna shake your tree.* You, too, love this song,
remember being 17, the urgent crossing
of state lines, the sweetest boy beside you,
how you both sang this dozens of times,
ate eggs and white toast at truck stops,
your bare feet resting on his thighs, the booth
your private place, chapel of possibility.
Both of you were certain then this sort
of freedom was pure covenant—plenty
of gas, decent meals, an unknown road,
someone to run with, forever, ever, amen.
You didn't think to be thankful. It was just eggs.

Visitor's Guide: Fort Churchill State Park

1860, and talk of Indian atrocities at Williams Station filtered back to Carson Valley settlers, who demanded immediate protection.

You may know where this is going, but keep in mind that the primary meaning of "to filter" is to pass something through a device to remove what's unwanted. "To filter" also means to assess items in order to reject those you don't want.

In July of that year, tens of thousands of dollars were spent to establish this desert outpost named after Sylvester Churchill, Inspector General of the U.S. Army. Sylvester was a distant relative of Winston Churchill. Note the resemblance in his portrait.

Strike a pose.

It was the so-called Pyramid Lake War that gave rise to this permanent installation of adobe buildings erected on stone in the form of a square, facing a central parade ground.

Gather, watch...

On May 12, 1860, three white men kidnapped and imprisoned two Indian girls. These three men were killed when Indians rescued the girls and burned the outpost. Rumors magnified the number of whites killed. Over a hundred volunteers rode to Pyramid Lake to avenge the deaths of white men. In the battle that ensued, the whites suffered a major defeat, losing two-thirds of their original force.

Let's do some math...

This decisive victory led to immediate white retaliation. In the second battle, the white majority forced retreat. Two whites died. Although casualty reports vary, up to 160 Indians were killed.

2 girls + 3 men + ? = ? Please take your time with this. This part of the exam matters.

The Visitor Center has exhibits which highlight the colorful history of Fort Churchill. Books, tee shirts, and ball caps are on sale.

Be sure to browse the children's section.
Reminder: DO NOT CLIMB ON THE RUINS. They are fragile.

Buckland Family Cemetery, Fort Churchill

SANFORD WILLIAM
Aged 1 Year & 8 Months

Here Rests the Sweetest Bud of Hope,
That Ere to Parents Wish Was Given.

CHARLES ADELBERT
Aged 8 Yrs. 8 Mo's. & 4 Days

He Suffered Long
But His Suffering's O'er
He Has Passed Away
Through The Golden Door.

ELIZA ANN
Aged 43 Yrs. 4 Mo's. & 2 Days

Shed Not For Her The Bitter Tear
Nor Give The Heart To Vain Regret
Tis But The Casket That Lies Here
The Gem That Filled It Sparkles Yet.

SAMUEL SANFORD BUCKLAND
Aged 58 years, 3 months – 15 days

Dear Is The Spot Where Our Father Sleeps
And Sweet The Strains The Angels Pour,
But Why Should We In Sorrow Weep,
He Is Not Lost But Gone Before.

The family of five recites these inscriptions out loud, carries the grandfather's wheelchair from grave to grave. The two children are hungry, but their parents are patient with the old man in the Korean Vet mesh cap, as patient as they can be. He wants to salute every stone, and the effort to raise him takes several grunting breaths. This is their last trip. Soon they'll drive into Silver Springs for hamburgers, scrambled eggs. The children won't remember this place, but they will remember that their grandfather liked his eggs soft, took a long time to swallow.

Day Trip to Lahontan

We plan to scatter smidgens of the dog
under trees, share the sandwiches we bought
at the Lahontan Market. In that quiet
parking lot, we met Rodney, retired,
now spends his good days riding in the bed
of his son-in-law's pickup truck, enthroned
on a cat-scratched recliner, beer in hand
dangling a string of walleye, a couple trout.

*

We find a shady spot along the lake,
spread our blankets, some ash, doze a little bit,
wake to the chatter of a young mother.
She's prepared for her three boys, two coolers
of cokes and snacks. The littlest one feeds
Cheetos to ring-billed gulls. His new favorite
word is *hate*. He *hates* the fish, his brothers,
he *hates* the warm soda, he *hates* the tight
life jacket. His mother reads a Bible.

*

On our way back to our campsite, we stop
again at the market, drawn by its two
Open signs, blinking string of Christmas lights,
orchestrated graffiti of smiley faces.
One of the bubbles says *Hi Cutie*, then
Not U Dude, another says *Kids Behave*.
We buy a six-pack and a sock monkey.
We've come to know the transience of joy.

Visitor's Guide: Rye Patch State Park

Thousands of years ago the Rye Patch area's climate was colder and wetter than it is now.

Stop for lunch in Lovelock. Try the Cowpoke Café where the Reuben is the bestseller. Eavesdrop on the tourists traveling I-80. Nearly every one of them will call home, wherever that might be, tell the person on the other end where they are, how it's the closest they'll ever get to O.J. Simpson. The waitress smiles, has heard this hundreds of times.

About 23,000 years ago when the elevation of the ancient lake was lower than the present reservoir, large animals such as camels, horses, mammoths and bison, as well as small rodents, came to drink from the springs in the riverbank. Some animals perished there.

If you skip the Cowpoke, drive in toward the park and try Gold Diggers Saloon and Grub House, where the sign promises "open most days most of the time." Have the fish and chips, tater tots smothered in nacho cheese sauce. Don't hold back. The bartender will join you for a couple of rounds, tell you that people from Italy have had her beer. She wants to be there.

Native people relied on hunting and gathering. They sometimes banded together on rabbit drives where nets hundreds of feet long were used to entangle the animals. They may have lived in groups as large as fifty during the winter and wandered the desert in much smaller groups during the summer.

And if you skip eating out, want to cook at your campsite, get groceries at the Safeway in Lovelock. Watch for the old man who wheels around the store with his little dog on his lap. You can't miss this—the dog wears sunglasses and a top hat. If you say something kind to the old man and his dog, the checker, her name is Clara, will give you the discount. You won't need a club card.

Rye Patch: Ranger Says

I used to work in Gardnerville, best
town I've ever lived in, but here's good,
pay's okay, and I got a baby boy on the way.
He's an oopsy, but as it gets closer
to his coming… gonna call him Porter.

The locals don't like me much, you might
meet some when they drive through after dark,
always wait till they think I'm in the house,
settled down to dinner, less likely to stop
them, get the park fee. I'm known as a hardass.

One guy wanted to pay his camping fee
with three quarters and a six-pack. Good beer.
A young couple from Kentucky tried to pay
with pretty rocks, like I don't see plenty
of pretty rocks. Let me think—

my best story is about the Playa Mates,
as they called themselves. Been at Burning Man,
this middle-aged guy and a teenaged girl
called their mating a marriage, and when
we got the call from a family of campers,

they were mating, that's for sure. We had to
arrest them for indecency, drove them
to the Pershing County Jail. By morning,
guy bails himself out, heads home to Seattle.
He left his bride behind. Stuff like that happens.

But if you really want to know the stories
of who's here or been here, check out the trash.
Garbage is the story. Look for what's left.

The Wildlife of Rye Patch

Familiar owl cry, duck honk, dove coo, rattle of raven, hawk screech, kee-kee of turkeys… quiet gaze of deer and wisp of cottontail. Owl again. Then they come…

First the locals from Winnemucca, taking the evening to fish. Bill works tomorrow, but tonight he's with his wife Stevie and their daughter Charmaine, stopping at our site to admire Roslyn, the *girliest little thing* they've ever seen. We talk dogs, of course, and finger the fine ash. They, too, have rescues, and Charmaine does love their *Mexican mix* and her purebred German shepherd. The shepherd came from Fallon, surrendered by a couple whose new baby had allergies, that's what they said. But Stevie's suspicious, thinks the baby *sucked all the affection those two could muster. It's so obvious*, she says. *That dog is hungry for love.* Bill says, *That dog's also a good kisser, but she's got prejudice. She doesn't like some folk, if you know what I mean, but thank goodness*, he says, *she loves her little sister.*

Next comes Albert from Battle Mountain, retired glazier. He's got hounds, his elderly mother, a boy of about fourteen. He's manning a 45-foot trailer, finds Roslyn a mystery of cute. This trailer is his baby, and he's got lots invested, a good six months of payments remain. He tells us this park is jumping on weekends, boaters and beer drinkers, and he's expecting his friends from town. When we ask if he's always lived in Battle Mountain, he says *Oh, no, I've been around. I've lived in Carson, Washoe Valley, Elko and Fallon. Winnemucca. As long as I can see this sky, even through a bit of window, I'm good.*

When Sam from San Francisco wanders over, it's nearly dark. He, too, is retired, a plumber by trade, and he's on his way to Cooperstown, his dream trip in his new rig. But first he's headed to Indiana where he'll pick up his high school buddy, take him along for the ride. This man still lives with his mother on a farm, and Sam, too, grew up there, son of a dairyman. He says he barely spoke English before he joined the Air Force, but now he knows a preposition from a participle. He says he owes the Air Force *everything*, all the ambition he came to embrace. He fought in Viet Nam with this same buddy, both of them released in June of '66, and he notes how much that date matters, *666*. He moved West, his buddy back home. Sam says he could get another job, even one here at this park, but he'd probably end up doing more plumbing, and *park shit has got to be bad*. He shows his arms, the burns from years of welding. Before he turns in, we share some beers. He says again, *I owe the Air Force everything. I knew nothing before. Back then, I had nowhere to go.*

Come morning, everyone is gone. We have coffee in the quiet, watch the deer along the river. But before we leave, Stevie's back, and she's brought a gift. Last night she made a big batch of her signature dish, Thundercloud Salad. Her aunts, grandmother, great grandmother passed this on, and she thought we might like some for the road home. When we ask about the recipe, she says,

> *First I let my cottage cheese hang out in a mesh strainer for 20-30 minutes. Then mix a jello packet with the cottage cheese and fold in a container of Cool Whip and strained fruit. I usually do orange jello with mandarin oranges or lime jello with pineapple. Then refrigerate. As far as measuring goes, I usually use the large of all three or the smaller of all three, hope that makes sense.*

This does make sense, makes senses make. Preposition. Place. Participle. Share. Owl. Deer. Dove. Stevie. Bill. Charmaine. Raven. Hawk. Turkey. Albert. Woman. Boy. Rabbit. Deer. Sam. Dear Sam…

PART TWO

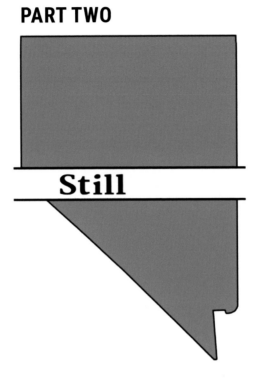

Still

Isabelle Steers: One thing about this town, it's always full of interesting strangers.

from *The Misfits*, 1961

Where Do You Go from Tonopah?

Because the Mizpah Hotel has claw foot tubs,
this is where you stop. This place has its own
ghost, a good story about The Lady in Red.
It's said she was murdered here, discovered
by her husband in the arms of her young love.
She'd have lived to wear her lace and heels
if it hadn't been for the train being late,
her husband missing his connection, stopping
in for a cold drink, seeing her, seeing him
ascend the steep stairs. In Nevada,
it's always about trains, drinks, connections
missed and made and wholly imagined.

Because, you're told, Tonopah is for those
with *a thirst for adventure*, you venture
into the Long Shot Bar, order steaks,
a fine red wine and, arguably, the best
margarita between Reno and Las Vegas,
listen to some old man chat up the young
couple from Henderson who say this is
the farthest north they've been, exploring
their new state, transplants from Atlanta.
The old man says *This is the real Nevada*,
but suggests they also make Elko, Winnemucca,
decent towns he's fond of, would live in, given…

And because you love books and the beauty
of dust, you'll spend hours wandering
the dense aisles of Whitney's Bookshelf,
where paperbacks are a dollar, hardbacks, two.
What you'll take home is a first edition,

hardback, John Gardner's *On Moral Fiction*.
Inside is a personal inscription, June 1978.
Bob, it says, *keep writing in NYC. Thanks*
for all your help these two years in Tonopah.
Best of luck. I'll miss you here. Love Jack.

Visitor's Guide: Wild Horse State Park

The reservoir was named after those that roamed abundantly in the area. Ranching has restricted the horses' movement, but they can still be found on the Owyhee Desert to the west.

Do you see?

The countryside is a treeless high and cold desert. Big sage dominates with patches of quaking aspen in the hills.

The trembling?

Although the park is open year-round, winter can be harsh. Spring and fall are unpredictable with the threat of winter weather at any moment.

Pay attention.

For more information during your visit, stop in at the Visitor Center. Hours will vary.

Note relative abundances.

Wild Horse: Ranger Says

So you want to talk to some campers?
Ask them about their dogs, seems like
everybody's got two or three. That's how
you meet people here. Just had a conversation
with a guy from Tucson, he's here to visit
his kids, they work in some mine in Elko.
He's the one with the mini dachshund. Dog's
name is Colter, guy was giving him a bath
at the fish cleaning station, thing no bigger
than a decent catch. I've no idea
what the man's name is, but he's headed next
to Colorado. That's the sort of talk
you'll get around here. It's good to keep moving.
That's why I'm here. You understand, don't you?

Of the Twelve Months of Beauty

We had a choice, drive the seventy miles
back to Elko for gas or take the canyon
into Owyhee. Elko tempted—the best
prime rib sandwiches at Machi's Saloon,
the heavy turquoise necklace at Capriola's
could be mine, I'd given it some thought.

So it was beef and beads or caramels, the candies
the ranger swears are worth the drive. We swerve
toward sweet, take the cattle-straddled route.
We're not alone. Tourists reach out car windows,
use their phones to capture the scene, the one
Nevada place most likely in calendars:
One of the twelve months of beauty.

On the Duck Valley Reservation, the Sho-Pai
tribes run Our Grocery Store where the caramels
are sold, lot full of Idaho plates waiting
to gas up. Two women who work the aisles
say they like my hat, and I imagine
some sort of trade, the hat for caramels,
for a gallon or two. I feel like
I'm in someone's movie, soundtrack

of trucks and wind. A yellow dog in a red
bandana lays her belly on the concrete
near the pumps, and when I reach for her,
she rolls onto her back, then slinks forward
for a pat, places her head between my legs.
If this were a movie, I'd take her,
let the audience imagine her fattened
and safe, a life of sweet treats and touch.

Back at Wild Horse, we stop at the ranger's
residence, plan to share our caramels,
thank him for sending us to Owyhee,
pockets of postcards and the skinny dog.
But he's not in. A note on his door reads
Gone to Elko for supplies. Long round trip.

Visitor's Guide: South Fork State Park

The South Fork of the Humboldt River originates along the west slope of the Ruby Mountains, approximately 40 miles south of Elko, Nevada.

Stop in Elko for lunch. Have the prime rib sandwich at Machi's Saloon, Wander over to Capriola's, take in the sex scent of leather, touch the silver. Buy something.

Plants include black sagebrush, rabbit brush, willow, rushes and forbs.

Smell the pot coming from the campsite downhill, the middle-aged men, call them Stan and Harvey, their long hair and full beards. Next morning they'll be gone, camp left nearly spotless, one spent roach under the picnic table.

Native trees are limited to narrow-leaf cottonwood, single-leaf pinyon pine and Utah juniper. Waterfowl include green-winged teal, American widgeon, northern shoveler, and common coots. Watch for Rocky Mountain mule deer, badgers and kit foxes.

Fishing and hunting in season with only a shotgun is allowed.

Listen. *Listen.*

South Fork: Ranger Says

Thank you. This is my favorite color
of lipstick, a punch of coral the shade
of salmon belly. It's made by Revlon
so you can find it at Walgreen's in Elko.
Lots of the men I've met here have also
noted my makeup, have found it worth
mentioning, and they do so with delight.
I guess some folks think that if you wear
a uniform and work outside here
in the fierce wind and unrelenting sun
you'd neglect your face, forego mascara,
a splash of scent, leave lips pale and dry.
But this is my place, and I honor it.
I live in my own trailer, move between
here and Lahontan on a Senior Pass.
Since I work here, I'm not required to buy
a pass, but it's only $30, and that's fair.
The state's raising the fees next year
so some seniors and vets will hurt,
will struggle, especially those who live
the life, move from park to park with their dogs,
all alone. Oh, yes, I know many of them
by name—Charley, Bob, Vernon, Billy, Hank…
I always look forward to seeing them,
but most have died, most of cancer, and some
don't come north anymore, too isolated,
too far from doctors. If I had to say,
I guess I miss Montana Mike the most.
He took to sitting in the sun all day.
He didn't look good last time I saw him.

I better get back to work now. Bob pulled
in last night, and I want to check on him.
You have a good time here, okay?
If you make a fire tonight, be careful.
This wind carries ash easily, and far.

Letter to Laura from South Fork

Allow me these Hugo moments, my own
little triggering towns. After your call,
in search of good wine, we drove into
Spring Creek, bought a case of Layer Cake
at Khoury's Market. You'd love the place
established nearly 40 years ago, the year
of your birth. The promise Gus and Sam
have made—*we will never ask you to ring
up or bag your own groceries*—

reminds us of our simpler pasts, how amazed
I was just hours ago to hear your voice
coming in clear from Amsterdam on this
sleepy Sunday. I remember the long wait
for Sundays, calls home to St. Louis
cheaper and, somehow, more meaningful.

Those were days of true long distance. I'd call
my father, catch him listening to his transistor
in the blistering square of his backyard,
Falstaff in hand, the sprinkler tearing
his tomatoes. We never spoke long.

Last night I listened to the Cardinals game
here where the Ruby Mountains tower
in the distance and the insistent wind
makes the cool of the Humboldt River true scent.
It was a close game. I should've called
my father, but the distance is long, still.

Did I tell you we bought carnations
at Khoury's Market? Spread some ashes
before we drank a bottle of the wine,
toasted you and your own adventure.
We wish you pure pleasure in your distance.

PART THREE

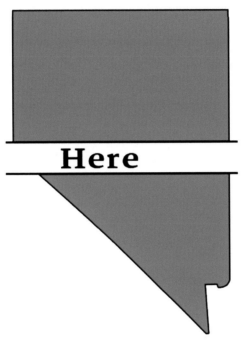

Here

Roslyn: We're all dying aren't we. We're not teaching each other what we really know, are we?

from *The Misfits,* 1961

Visitor's Guide: Kershaw-Ryan State Park

Early settlers cultivated a garden of grapes, orchards and vegetables for sale to the miners in nearby Pioche.

You'll want to meet Herman. He's a retired lineman, has lived in Pioche for 54 years. The kids are grown, and the first thing they did was leave. He's gardened this park for five years, keeps the 27-year-old koi alive in the little pond, something wedding parties like to see, will dangle their fingers above the water, reach in to touch. He tends the grapes, the apple, pear and plum trees. Gardening is a good thing, quiet. And he gets to make beauty, he says, knows each of the 200 plants in the greenhouse. He doesn't know anyone in Pioche anymore.

In Kershaw Canyon, Horse Springs channeled into a trough where wild horses and deer came to water. Mountain lions, bobcats, foxes and coyotes also frequent this area. Reptiles, too.

You'll also want to meet Frank. He's the camp host, lives in the park year-round. He's divorced, originally from Bishop, California, a family of masons. His kids live in Dayton now, and it's hard to visit, too intense, the stress of traffic and noise. Everything aches. But his shoulders begin to relax on the return trip when he hits Tonopah. It's about feeling safe. Frank keeps a water bowl under his camper, is sometimes visited by a mountain lion he's come to call Shirley. She won't visit if there are campers, only comes to see him. They once shared a lunch of fried chicken. Only days later did he realize what could've happened, the strong stealth of Shirley. But nothing happened. Not then. Not yet.

Shady Motel, Caliente, Nevada

This is a real place, you text to friends,
advertises itself as *Stress Free*,
if you like the sounds of passing trains
barking dogs, the rumble of big rigs.
And you do like these things, chose this motel
for the view of the historic depot,
the easy drive down to the state parks.
You feel safe here, you've got some of your own
dog with you, everyone who sits outside
smokes, some claim to be charmed by the irony
of the motel's name, the nearly complete
lack of shade, the unforgiving heat.

You'll dinner at the Knotty Pine, fried chicken,
mashed potatoes so honest the lumps
are the same size as the peas you swirl
into them. Two beers into your meal, you'll buy t-shirts,
text the same friends the evidence—*Knotty Boys*
in XL, *Knotty Girls* in medium and small.

After eating, you'll walk the full length
of Caliente, admire the Mission Revival
architecture of the depot, note the many
shuttered stores on the north end of town.
When you come to the Hot Springs Motel,
a sudden breeze will find you, and you'll text
how unnatural that moment was,
the chill, the certain drop, the swift of shade.
This most alive mystery occurs weeks
before you learn that this motel is where,

in Room 15, always in Room 15,
Warren Jeffs married off teen girls, not far

at all from your safe, sated, shady place.

At the Elgin Schoolhouse,
You Remember Tanisha

You'll want to make a reservation, take
a private tour with the ranger. He knows
how to tell a decent story, how until this
one-room schoolhouse, the youth of Elgin
were home-schooled, Panaca a good 36
miles north, too far a wagon ride for hauling
children. From 1922 till 1967, this place
took Elgin residents through eighth grade,
enough education for some of them, those
who'd stay, work the San Pedro railroad
or deliver telegrams to sidings for Western Union.

If you'd lived here, this is where you'd have read
about Sally, Dick, and Jane, fallen in love
with Puff, learned to pledge allegiance, recite
Bible verses, learned to sit still, be quiet.
All the books are still here, you can touch them,
see the long ruler on the teacher's desk,
her teacup. She'd have been content here,
a good job, housing included. She'd stay
until the young rancher, his hat in hand,
persuaded her to marry. You'd miss her,
wonder, on occasion, if she lived *happily*...

*

The Caliente Youth Center lies 22 miles
north of Elgin. It, too, nestles against
mountains, suggests serenity, hope,
a nearly holy beauty of promise.
This is Nevada's lockdown high school,

where boys and girls who've got nothing left
come to, as the brochure states, find purpose
in a community of correctional care.
You met Tanisha there, came to teach storytelling
to those who owned stories worth telling.
Tanisha thought you looked like a movie star,
envied your high heels, embroidered denim jacket.
Her state-issued gray sweats were bloodstained.

You tried to teach a little poetry,
encouraged emotional honesty,
made suggestions about imagery,
about rhythm. Tanisha wrote four
haiku, each one devoted to her lust
for a boy in a neighboring unit,
imagined their life safe and meaningful.
You hoped to take her deeper, but someone
brought a shiv to class, the alarms loud
and insistent all students march outdoors.
You were dismissed. But still, on occasion,
you'll think of Tanisha, whose name means
happiness, means *ambition*. And you'll wonder.

The Infrequent, Yet Beautiful, Trumpeters

are swans, seen rarely but always a wonder
at Spring Valley State Park, Pioche, Nevada.
The park's visitor guide heralds the birds,
says campers and hikers share the canyons
with eagles, hawks, herons, avocets, and yes,
the infrequent, yet beautiful, trumpet swan.
It's the *yet* that puzzles, suggests that strangers
are more exquisite than regulars,
a theory you intend to challenge
in the dark bar of the Overland Hotel.

The bartender's name is Dakota,
and she makes a mean Bloody Mary.
A sizzler with green beans, pepperoni slice,
it's a salad in a tumbler. You'll have two
before you buy a couple of cows, porcelain,
one wearing a red bow, the other dangling
earrings, not unlike those you once lost.
As you consider ordering a third drink
or leaving to cross the street for burgers
at the Ghost Town Art & Coffee Co.,
where a retired rocker hand pats the meat,
grills it over coals out back, a tourist takes
the stool on your left, a regular takes
the right. The tourist is from Boulder City,
and it's her first visit to Pioche. She's okay
with the smokers, says she used to smoke
Marlboro Lights, then went on a menthol binge
until a new husband made her give it all up.
She's curious about a sign behind the bar:
No pipes, cigars, or aromatic cigarettes—
Aren't all smokes aromatic, she asks,
and isn't that the point? The regular

orders beer and a shot, pulls a photo
of a young man with a mullet cut
and a wide grin of bucked teeth, pulls it from
his shirt pocket, places it face up,
closes his eyes, raises both glasses in toast.
When others who seem to frequent this place
trickle in, they pat his back, squeeze his arm,
raise their own glasses. Nothing is said.

You'll have that third drink, think again about
the infrequent, yet beautiful, trumpeters,
how some songs are best heard loudly, others
in a shadowed, quiet place. There's surely
a frequency of pain, of grief, of pure
and abundant disaster everywhere.
Yet, for now, most of that is outside.
In here the sin is sweet. It's beautiful.

Visitor's Guide: Cathedral Gorge State Park

Two thousand acres once home to Southern Paiutes, claimed glorious and named by a white woman. Mrs. Earl Godbe, awed by the sculpted landscape, her memory of European cathedrals. For years, residents of a nearby mining camp staged Biblical pageants inside the narrow canyons, their song a hallowing of beauty, of possession.

Tread, tread.

If you were in the Gorge 2.5 million years ago, you would have needed gills. Be on the lookout for lizards and black-tailed jackrabbits. In the evenings and early mornings, watch for kangaroo rats, kit foxes, mule deer. You may catch a glimpse of a golden eagle or the state's Mountain Bluebird. Brightly colored gopher snakes are common, an occasional Great Basin Rattlesnake.

Tread lightly.

Look for dark, bumpy patches around rocks. This is Cryptobiotic soil, alive with mosses, algae, microfungi, bacteria. These microcosms are fragile, easily damaged when disturbed, can take 100 years to recover.

Tread lightly, lightly, lightly.

A photographer's dream, the park offers stunning views of the canyons and caves. Do see Moon Canyon, where under a full moon, the lighter-toned cliffs will glow.

You can also, like the family from Virginia, take photos from your car window, drive through quickly, stay on the roads, put your check mark next to this attraction, say you've seen the Real West, been Out There. You'll miss the Oakbrush Sumac, the Antelope Bitterbrush, the Fourwing Saltbrush, the Utah Juniper, and the Insect Galls. But you'll certainly possess some pretty pictures. And you won't even have to tread. Not one bit.

Cathedral Gorge: Ranger Says

You're right—this is the perfect place to honor
a dog, spread ashes, leave bone. I'm sorry
for your loss. Dog's name was Miller, you said?
Take some of his ashes up to Miller Point.
Seems perfect. And did you see the plaque
under the juniper along the Nature Loop?
Dog's name was Herbie, inscription says
Best Dog Ever. Don't know who set that plaque,
but I like it. That dog was surely loved.

I've been here 18 years, right out of high school,
married the prettiest girl in Panaca.
She tends bar at the Knotty Pine in Caliente.
You should check it out, it's right down the street
from the Shady Motel. We have a good life here.

But years have changed things in this park,
now that there's electric service at nearly
every site. Tenters are disadvantaged,
need to build fires for warmth and cooking,
and then those in the fancy campers complain,
say they're getting smoked out. It gets ugly.
And the Europeans walk around nude, take
showers in full view. That can be ugly, too.
Or beautiful. Depends on perspective.

Listen, I've got some dog cookies in the shop.
You could crumble them, leave with the ashes.
Let me know what you need. I'm always here.

Man, Dog, Daughter, Jesus

He sits outside his battered RV, wearied
after his fourth trip to the wood pile.
At four dollars an armload,
this detail suggests he's planning
on more than a night or two. He builds
his first fire in the March chill, brings out
the fraying lawn chair, the one with stars
patterned in red, white, blue, not quite
an American flag, but close. Real close.
He's got an equally old Border Collie,
at least in dog years, and at dusk,
the onions chopped, the burgers grilled,
the blessed scent of baked potato easy
in the crisp air, he feeds the dog by hand.
Let's call the man John. Let's call the dog Lucky.

John's rig has Arkansas license plates,
so I wander over, tell him I came from
the *Land of Opportunity*, the state's
old and retired motto. We recollect,
tell stories about what makes Arkansas
so very pretty but nothing like this
celestial Nevada landscape, its haunt,
its openness, how the space both reveals
and conceals. I'm here by choice. John's here
to find his daughter, gone now near forty
years. He hasn't much time left and even
Lucky is old and declining. John could be
my own father, if mine had come down
from the hills, had taken me into Eureka
Springs to show me the imposing statue,
Christ of the Ozarks. A reverent afternoon—
lunch in a little bistro, hushpuppies
the size of tennis balls. It's there,

in the soft booth, a place of cloth napkins
and heavy flatware, that I decide to leave.
The tourists are laughing, drinking, they're here
to see the seven-story Jesus, third tallest
in the world, two million pounds of steel and mortar.
Their voices are filled with light, confidence,
amusement. They find humor in big Jesus,
and that's what I want, a life that allows
for irony, a life lived in places
from which one tours, finds quiet America
a diversion, a place best seen briefly.
Perhaps I make my way to Las Vegas,
an act of impulsive courage, or maybe
I go to Reno, city of compromise.

But this isn't my story. This is about
John, about Lucky, about their search
for a middle-aged woman one remembers
as a good girl, the other has never known.
John's driven through Tulsa, Albuquerque,
as far north as Omaha, places she once
said out loud. Tomorrow, Sin City.
He hopes she's not there. He hopes she's looking
for him, finds him sitting in his festive chair.
He'd set off some fireworks, sparklers
she used to love. He prays for that day.
Lucky just puts his chin against paw, and from
somewhere deep within his small but surely
sacred heart, comes a keening I know too well.

Visitor's Guide: Berlin-Ichthyosaur State Park

Here's a tip: before you venture out, practice saying the park's name. Revel in the way your mouth moves, the way the hardness twists your face, rolls around your tongue. This hardness is essential to understand.

Ichthyosaurs were prehistoric marine reptiles, the most highly specialized reptile to have ever lived on earth. They bore their young alive, had amazingly large eyes. Found on all continents except Antarctica, their widespread existence and apparent success make their extinction all the more mysterious.

During its heyday, the Berlin Mine's total production is estimated to have been $849,000, at a time when gold was $20 per ounce. Berlin is now a true ghost town, at its height in 1908, declining to its death in 1911.

Pretty is as pretty does? What price beauty?

Over 40 ichthyosaurs have been discovered at various locations throughout the park and are among the largest specimens known. These are dubbed *Shonisaurus populatis*, named after the Shoshone mountain range. Today *Shonisaurus populatis* is the Nevada State fossil.

Berlin once supported over 200 people: miners, woodcutters, charcoal makers, a doctor, a nurse, a forest ranger, and a prostitute. The buildings they lived and worked in are maintained in a state of arrested decay.

Watch for snakes. Be sure to tour the fossil house. You can buy a stuffed ichthyosaur. It's the softest thing you'll hold here.

Postcard: Highway 50 Shoe Tree

—a found poem with commentary

As the story goes, newlyweds started this. They got into an argument, she intended to walk home, he said, "You do and you'll have to go barefoot" and he threw her shoes into the 80 foot cottonwood along the stretch of Nevada's highway. Over a decade later the tree is a footware phenomenon, its branches bearing hundreds of shoes. The tree sit between Austin and Fallon Nevada near Middlegate Station along U.S. 50, the loneliest road in America. Good thing shoes come in pairs, they can keep each other company! Sadly some vandal cut this wonderful tree down Dec. 31st 2010, the sister tree now stands proudly nearby ready to take up the chore, shoes by the hundreds have already decorated her limbs. The nearby stump still reminds us of the once regal tree.

*

A middle-aged couple on a good-sized Harley, Michigan plate, stops at the Shoe Tree turnoff. He says, *This is kinda stupid. I suppose it's art? I don't get it.* She says, *It's what they call an installation.* He says, *I still don't get it. I just don't.*

Overheard at Middlegate Station, Known as "The
Real Old West on Lonely Highway 50," While Waiting
Over an Hour for a BLT, Surrounded by Tourists
Clamoring for a Table

I thought the map said *Loveliest* Road in America.

Red, White, Blue, Pink, and Blue Again

On the final night of your stay, you'll walk
the loop of Berlin-Ichthyosaur to check
out who's pulled in. You're beginning
to feel like these remote parks belong
to you, know you'll return, of course,
to visit the secret spots where you've left
ash of the dead dog. You'll also return
just to hear the human sounds, how voices
carry in quiet places when people
think nobody's listening. But you are.

Listen to the two little girls on their pink
bikes, purple tires with matching streamers.
They whisk by you as you walk, they are chanting
Red, White, Blue, We Love You! The youngest
is wearing red cowboy boots, a straw hat.
Last night they walked with their father, an old
dog limping along behind them, the dog's
slipping hip painful to see. Last night, no
chanting, but they did recite the Pledge
Of Allegiance, over and over and over.

Listen to the large party from Storey County
who's set up satellite dishes, blast
country music, Randy Travis. You haven't
thought of Randy Travis in years, once
loved his voice of velvet and pearl.
They are roasting chicken, will invite
their nearest neighbor to join them,
the gray-haired woman from Texas
who wears sweatpants under a batik housedress.

Listen to the woman from Goldfield, where
she's lived the last five years with her family
of two kids, two dogs. She's telling the man
from Minden how they lived in their 5th Wheel
for four years, and as she speaks, she swings
her long hair, long enough to sit on. The man
says he's a native, born in '42 in Saint Mary's.
He'll leave her a Rotary Club card, wish her well.

On this last night of your pilgrimage,
you'll drink lots of red wine, grill steaks
you know would bring the old dog running.
From somewhere in the park you hear
the crackle of radio, know the rangers
are making their last rounds, will wave.
Soon the sweet smell of dying fires will ease
you toward your own rest. The last voice
you'll hear is one singing, barely a whisper.

What We Carried Home

From Washoe City, girl's fabric bracelet, little roses in purple bunches.

From Dayton, photo of Misfits Flats.

From Fallon, sock monkey.

From Silver Springs, four donkey planters from Occupied Japan.

From Battle Mountain, carton of cigarettes.

From Winnemucca, thrift store suede jacket with blue fringe.

From Lovelock, plastic flask with a sugar skull face.

From Tonopah, Gardner's *Art of Fiction* and *Beef Cattle Science*, a textbook, two wine glasses from the Mizpah Hotel bar.

From Spring Creek, keychain with silver fish and a case of wine.

From Elko, chunky turquoise necklace.

From Owyhee, box of caramels.

From Caliente, t-shirts from the Knotty Pine bar.

From Panaca, yet more t-shirts, refrigerator magnets, a Cathedral Gorge coffee mug.

From Pioche, porcelain cattle, a Silver Café coffee mug.

From Berlin, rocks painted with dinosaurs, a stuffed ichthyosaur.

From Middlegate, postcard of the original Shoe Tree.

One empty paint can.

Notes

This work is a product of both imagination and observation. Most of the names of people I encountered throughout the state of Nevada have been altered.

The "Visitor's Guide" poems use found, manipulated and created language. Some of the language in these pieces comes from the brochures available at each park. Changes in typeface indicate the moves between borrowed and created language. The *Ranger Says* poems use both actual stories rangers told me and imagined context for those stories.

"Note to Willy from Dayton" references writer Willy Vlautin, a Nevada native and one helluva great guy. His most recent novel is *Don't Skip Out on Me*, and it's a must-read.

"Of the Twelve Months of Beauty" references an actual calendar with a similar title. Also referenced is Tammen Tameeh Kahni, the tribal-owned and run grocery store in Owyhee, Nevada. The English translation of the store's name is Our Grocery Store, and this also appears on all the signage, and for the purposes of this project, using the English translation seemed more appropriate for the voice and perspective of the poem itself.

"Letter to Laura from South Fork" is for poet Laura Wetherington, who moved to the Netherlands with her family after the 2016 election. Also referenced is the late poet and teacher Richard Hugo, whose books *The Triggering Town* and *31 Letters and 13 Dreams* continue to be among those that most inspire my own work.

"The Beautiful, Yet Infrequent, Trumpeters" borrows part of a line from Roy Bentley's poem "Our Local Heavens," which appears in his book *Walking with Eve in the Loved City*. Read the poem. Read the whole book.

The lines of Gay, Guido, Roslyn, and Isabelle Speers are from the movie *The Misfits*. Directed by John Huston, written by Arthur Miller, and filmed in Reno and northern Nevada, this 1961 film was the last completed by Clark Gable (Gay) and Marilyn Monroe (Roslyn). The film also stars Thelma Ritter as Isabelle, Eli Wallach as Guido, and Montgomery Clift as Perce. This film is quintessential Nevada—it's both brutal and beautiful. It will break your heart.

Acknowledgments

I am profoundly indebted to the Nevada Arts Council (NAC), the agency that encouraged and supported this work by granting me a Major Project Fellowship. The proposal was that I would travel from my home base of Reno out into the more rural and remote places of Nevada, spending two to three days in various state parks, where I would gather ideas for poems and vignettes. Without the support of the NAC, this project and the rich experiences it allowed me would not have been possible. I'm particularly beholden to Fran Morrow, NAC's Artists Services Specialist. Without Fran's encouragement and guidance, even the proposal for this project may never have been envisioned.

Thanks to Kirk Robertson and Valerie Serpa of Churchill Arts Council; Bobbie Ann Howell of Nevada Humanities; Christine Kelly of Sundance Bookstore; and Jennifer Dawson, Ranger at Washoe Lake State Park for writing support letters for this project. Christine and Valerie, extra gratitude for hosting readings in Reno and Fallon while this work was in progress. And Jen, thank you for introducing me to the beauty of Washoe Lake and for the much-appreciated introductions to other rangers throughout Nevada State Parks.

Thanks to David Lee, Eleanor Wilner, and everyone involved with the Cliff Notes Writers Conference in Boulder, Utah, where a reading of this work was debuted. I most appreciate your enthusiastic support. As Eleanor said, "What a great assignment… to have a state pass through the mouth of a poet—now that is the best use of government money I can imagine."

Thanks to the editors of *Manzano Mountain Review*, where some of these poems originally appeared.

Thanks to Caitlin McCarty, Artistic Director of Collateral & Co. Contemporary Dance Company, and all the dancers and choreographers in her company. Thanks to all of you for creating both *Dust Horizon* and *Dust Settled*, two full-length dance programs inspired by my work. The performances at the Nevada Museum of Art and during Reno's Artown celebration were most certainly the icing for this project.

And thank you, Don, for just about everything. Without whom…

And lastly, Miller. You were the best dog ever.

About the Author

Gailmarie Pahmeier has lived most of her life in Nevada. She teaches creative writing in the MFA Programs at Sierra Nevada University and the University of Nevada, where she has been honored with various teaching awards, including the University Distinguished Teacher Award.

Widely published, her work has received a number of awards, including a Witter Bynner Poetry Fellowship, an Academy of American Poets Prize, and three fellowships from the Nevada Arts Council. It was the prestigious and competitive Major Project Fellowship from the Nevada Arts Council which funded the travel and research for this project.

Pahmeier is the author of three chapbooks and two full-length collections of poetry, including *The Rural Lives of Nice Girls*. In 2015, she was appointed Reno's first Poet Laureate, in 2016 she was inducted into the Nevada Writers Hall of Fame, and in 2017, she was selected as Nevada's Outstanding Teacher in the Humanities.

.